BEING A SENCO

BEING A SENCO

{ Lynn How }

3rd Floor
HYLO
103–105 Bunhill Row
London, EC1Y 8LZ
UK

2455 Teller Road
Thousand Oaks
California 91320

10th Floor, Emaar Capital Tower
2 MG Road, Sikanderpur, Sector 26
Gurugram, Haryana – 122002

8 Marina View Suite 43-053
Asia Square Tower 1
Singapore 018960

Editor: James Clark
Editorial assistant: Harry Dixon
Production editor: Sarah Cooke
Marketing manager: Lucy Sofroniou
Cover design: Wendy Scott
Typeset by: C&M Digitals (P) Ltd, Chennai, India
Printed in the UK by Bell & Bain Ltd, Glasgow
BB0364363

British Library Cataloguing in Publication data

A catalogue record for this book is available from the British Library

ISBN 978-1-0362-4125-4 (pbk)

TABLE OF CONTENTS

{ ABOUT THIS BOOK }

Stepping into the role of SENCO can feel both exciting and overwhelming. This short guide is designed to offer practical support, helping you navigate the realities of the role with greater confidence and clarity. Drawing on real experience from schools, it focuses on what actually matters day to day: supporting pupils with SEND, working effectively with staff and families, and building inclusive practice across your school.

- Written by an experienced SENCO and educational consultant working in schools
- Practical, realistic guidance you can apply straight away
- Short sections that are easy to dip in and out of when time is limited
- Reflection prompts to help you shape the role in a way that works for you and your setting

Read it in an all at once for a helpful overview or return to different sections as questions arise throughout your SENCO journey.

Find out more at
www.sagepub.co.uk/littleguides

a little guide for teachers

{ ABOUT THE SERIES }

The **A LITTLE GUIDE FOR TEACHERS** series is little in size but big on all the support and inspiration you need to navigate your day-to-day life as a teacher.

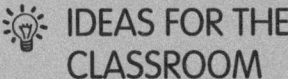
IDEAS FOR THE CLASSROOM

REFLECTION POINT

HINTS & TIPS

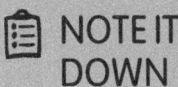
NOTE IT DOWN

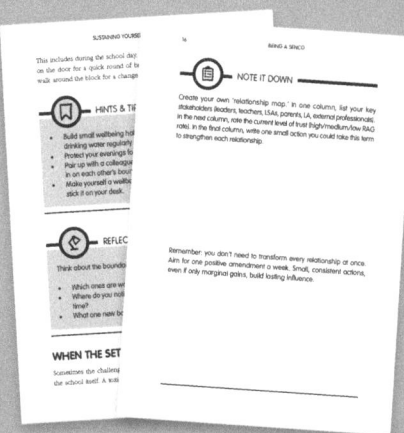

www.sagepub.co.uk/littleguides

ABOUT THE AUTHOR

Lynn How is a SENCo, educational consultant, SEND mum, trainer and author with over 24 years of experience working across primary education in a wide range of roles, including class teacher, assistant headteacher and ITT lead mentor. She currently works with schools, trusts and individuals across the UK, supporting inclusive practice, SEND leadership and staff wellbeing.

Lynn is known for her honest, practical and down-to-earth approach to SENCoing. She specialises in helping schools embed high-quality teaching for pupils with SEND, develop confident SENCo leadership, and create systems that are both effective and sustainable. Alongside her consultancy and public speaking work, she delivers training, webinars and coaching for SENCos and school leaders, drawing on her real-world (and current) SENCo experiences.

She runs Positive Young Minds, a platform dedicated to SEND, inclusion and educator wellbeing, and leads one of the UK's largest online SENCo communities 'The Sweary SENCo', which puts SENCo wellbeing at the heart of practice. Through her writing, training and online presence, Lynn is a strong advocate for putting the practitioner first, recognising that inclusive schools depend on supported, confident and healthy SENCos.

Lynn has written for a range of educational organisations and publications and has appeared on SEND-focused podcasts and webinars. She supports Teacher Toolkit and works with Kindness Matters to promote compassionate, inclusive school cultures.

She holds an MA in Education, is a Fellow of the Chartered College of Teaching, and holds the NASENCo qualification and NPQH.

All resources and links can be found at: **https://linktr.ee/ positiveyoungmind**

ACKNOWLEDGEMENTS

This book exists because of you.

It is for the SENCos who keep going when the system feels stacked against them. The ones juggling impossible workloads, impossible expectations and impossible timelines, while still showing up for children, families and colleagues with care and professionalism, all alongside juggling their own family lives.

I want to thank every practitioner in my Sweary SENCo network. Your honesty, humour, frustrations and relentless determination have shaped this book more than you may realise. The questions you ask, the stories you share and the support you offer one another remind me daily that SENCoing is not a solo role, even when it can feel painfully isolating.

Thank you for your tenacity, your resilience and for sharing your experiences so openly whilst supporting one another without judgement, and for continuing to fight for inclusion in a system that often makes that far harder than it should be.

This book is for you, and because of you. We are stronger together.

ABBREVIATIONS

APDR	Assess, Plan, Do, Review
ARE	Age-related Expectations
CPD	Continuing Professional Development
ECTs	Early Careers Teachers
EEF	Education Endowment Foundation
EHCNA	Education, Health and Care Needs Assessment
EHCP	Education, Health and Care Plan
EP	Educational Psychologist
GPT	Generative Pre-trained Transformer
HT	Head Teacher
IEP	Individual Education Plan
IPRA	Individual Pupil Resourcing Agreement
IPSEA	Independent Provider of Special Education Advice
LA	Local Authority
LAC	Looked-after Children
LSA	Learning Support Assistant
MAT	Multi-Academy Trusts
NASEN	National Association for Special Educational Needs
NASENCo	National Award for SEN Co-ordination
OT	Occupational Therapist
QFT	Quality First Teaching
RAG	Red, Amber, Green
SaLTs	Speech and Language Therapists
SATS	Standard Assessment Tests

SEDAL	Social-Emotional Developmental Age Level
SEMH	Social, Emotional, and Mental Health
SEND	Special Educational Needs and Disabilities
SENCo	Special Educational Needs Coordinator
SLT	Senior Leadership Team
TA	Teaching Assistant
YARC	York Assessment of Reading for Comprehension

INTRODUCTION

The role of SENCo has never been more important – or more complex. Across the UK, schools are facing rising levels of need, ever-tighter budgets, staff shortages, and the pressure of external scrutiny. All alongside a new White Paper and OFSTED framework. Against this backdrop, SENCos find themselves pulled in many directions, including coordinating support, leading staff, supporting families, and trying to stay afloat personally.

I wish to begin by acknowledging that reality. I don't want to minimise the challenges, nor do I want to paint an apocalyptic picture. To deny the challenges would feel disingenuous, but to dwell only on them risks leaving us feeling defeated. The truth sits somewhere in the middle: while the pressures are very real, so too is the resilience, creativity, and compassion that exists within schools. In fact, some schools are thriving despite the difficulties – not because the problems have disappeared, but because they've found ways to work differently, together.

What I hope to offer here is not another checklist of everything you 'should' be doing (your to-do list is long enough). Instead, this is a companion for your journey as a SENCo: honest, practical, and hopefully a little reassuring. Each chapter shares lessons I learnt – often the hard way – alongside strategies you can try, reflect on, or adapt for your context. Think of this book more like a conversation with a colleague who understands the chaos, has made plenty of mistakes along the way, and is happy to share what worked and what didn't.

Throughout these pages, you'll see reflection points and activities designed for you to jot down your own thoughts to support you in shaping your role in a way that is both effective for your school and sustainable for you.

When I first became a SENCo, I thought the hardest part would be mastering the law, the paperwork, the acronyms. Don't get me wrong – those things matter, but I quickly realised they weren't the real challenge. The real challenge was navigating relationships, supporting staff who were struggling, keeping parents on side, and somehow finding time to look after myself in sometimes challenging circumstances. If that resonates with you, then you're in the right place.

This little guide isn't designed to cover *everything* about the SENCo role. Instead, it's designed to support you with the essentials – the parts of the role that make the biggest difference to your effectiveness and wellbeing. Each chapter focuses on a core area, offering strategies, reflection points, and activities you can use straight away.

Most importantly, this book is about you. Too often, professional development materials focus solely on what we should be doing for students. Of course, that's vital – but unless SENCos are supported, confident, and well, we can't do our best work for anyone else. So, consider this your space to pause, reflect, and re-think how you approach your role in a way that's both effective and sustainable.

As you read, you'll notice opportunities to stop and reflect, to jot down thoughts, or to try out an activity. Use these in a way that works for you. It is my hope that you take something practical away, whether that's a fresh perspective, a new strategy, or simply the reassurance that you're not alone.

So, whether you're brand new to the role or years into it, thank you for choosing to spend some time with this book. I wish to provide clarity, encouragement, and – just as importantly – a reminder of why SENCoing (from my clearly biased perspective), is the most rewarding job in education.

Also, any free resources suggested in this book are discoverable on my website: **https://positiveyoungmind.com/senco-resources/**

CHAPTER 1
THE POWER OF RELATIONSHIPS: BUILDING TRUST AND INFLUENCE

This chapter will explore:

- Building trust and credibility across the school
- Being visible and approachable in your setting
- Communicating clearly under pressure
- Navigating difficult dynamics with staff, parents, and external professionals

INTRODUCTION

If there's one lesson my years as a SENCo and senior leader have taught me, it's this: relationships matter more than paperwork. The mountains of paperwork will always be there but unless you can build trust with the people around you, those forms won't translate into real support for children.

> *People do not care how much you know until they know how much you care.*
> *John C. Maxwell (1989: p6)*

The SENCo role often feels like standing at the centre of a broken set of traffic lights, with cars coming at you from every direction – leaders, teachers, parents, local authority officers, therapists, and, of course, the students themselves. You're not in control of the traffic but you have been delegated to direct it and expected to keep it moving smoothly. That's only possible if you build the kinds of connections that mean people trust you enough to follow your lead, listen to your advice, or simply pick up the phone when you need them.

This chapter will explore the central role of relationships in SENCoing, drawing on practical strategies and plenty of reflection. It will also give you space to pause and think about how you might strengthen your own network of influence – because in this job, no SENCo is an island.

BUILDING TRUST AND CREDIBILITY ACROSS THE SCHOOL

Trust takes time, and as a SENCo, you don't always get the luxury of easing into relationships, especially if you join a new school (congratulations if you have a new job!). Staff will expect you to know things straight away. Parents will expect you to have answers. Leaders will expect you to deliver outcomes. You can concurrently hope that you will have the resources to be able to handle these expectations effectively, but we all know that this often not the case! Therefore going out of your way to build those relationships does a lot to 'grease the communication wheels' when the going gets tough.

One of the simplest but most effective ways to build credibility is visibility. If colleagues only ever see you when something goes wrong, they'll associate you with problems rather than support.

- Drop into classrooms regularly for five minutes just to see what's happening and be friendly – eventually you'll be a welcome part of the furniture.
- Share quick wins in staff briefings – a helpful resource, a new strategy, or just a positive story (bear in mind some members of staff hate public praise – check before you name!).
- Make yourself available in small, informal ways: a chat in the corridor can sometimes be more effective than a formal meeting – although systems need to be in place, such as concern sheets, (which are on my website), so that you don't forget the conversation and suggested actions.

Trust also grows when you admit what you don't know. Early in my SENCo career, I thought credibility came from having all the answers and at the time; I was overwhelmed with learning the role! What I now understand is that people respected me more when I said, 'I don't know right now, but I'll find out and come back to you.'

REFLECTION POINT 1.1

- Think about your own visibility in school. Where and how do colleagues most often see you?
- Do they associate you with support, solutions, or stress?
- How does this fit in with the culture of your school (for example, do other SLT members' visibility incite stress, if so, how can you improve this for your role)?

BEING VISIBLE AND APPROACHABLE

It's so easy (and sometimes necessary) to spend hours locked away in an office trying to get through the paperwork mountain. At times when I have done this, the problem is, staff can't see the hours I am putting in – all they see is a closed door. I know that being approachable is as important as being efficient. It's a delicate balance.

Practical ideas for visibility and efficiency:

- Holding a weekly 'open door' slot where staff know they can drop in.
- Sitting in the staffroom regularly.
- Visiting LSAs in their classrooms rather than always calling them to you.
- Sharing your roles and responsibilities at the start of each year so that staff understand the breadth of your role, what both you and they are responsible for and where there is overlap.

It's not about being available 24/7 – boundaries matter and a 'Do not disturb' sign or the ability to work from home is entirely appropriate at times. But if you want colleagues to share concerns early rather than waiting for a crisis, they need to see you as someone who is accessible.

IDEAS FOR THE CLASSROOM 1.1

Create your own 'Do not disturb' sign

You may want to have a sign for your door for when you need to focus on tasks without interruption. What would you put on your sign?

Ideas include:

Please don't disturb Mrs How unless:

- Aliens have landed
- You have cake (must be good cake)
- A cat is in the playground

WHEN RELATIONSHIPS FEEL STRAINED: STAFF AND PARENTS

Not every relationship will be smooth. *That* colleague may see SEND as 'your job' and resist making adjustments and expect you to come running with every issue (of course, some whole school CPD is also needed for this issue…). A top tip here is to find out what that colleague's hobbies are, show an interest in their family and life and strike up a conversation. Usually works with school leaders as well…

From a parent perspective, some parents may arrive defensive or angry because of 'the last straw' – often because they've had to fight to be heard in the past and getting SEND support and funding is increasingly challenging.

A mantra that helped me is 'Frustration is usually fear in disguise.' A teacher may fear being judged if they admit they're struggling. A parent may fear their child will be overlooked. An LSA may fear they're not skilled enough.

When I began looking for the fear beneath the frustration, it changed the way I responded. Instead of becoming defensive, I could show empathy and ask: 'What's the biggest worry for you right now?' Most people simply want to be heard, and if you can provide that supportive space, often they leave much happier, even if you haven't been able to provide exactly what they want. I often consider what it would be like to live in these people's lives.

> *You never really understand a person until you consider things from his point of view... until you climb into his skin and walk around in it.*
> *Harper Lee (1989: p30)*

Although this act would be somewhat extreme, the sentiment is always there. For this reason, I even invented a new word, *comprathy,* for when empathy is just not enough, after trying to relate to one of my best friend's challenging lived experiences which were vastly different to my own. It was also inspired by all of those families I've supported over the years, such as Sam who had cerebral palsy and epilepsy, meaning that the learning had difficulty sticking, or Ahmed who had a genetic condition that rendered all the boys in his family blind – I couldn't imagine living a week with their particular circumstances, let alone a lifetime. Comprathy is a step further from empathy, acknowledging that you have no frame of reference to understand what someone's life or issue is like. Learn more here: **www.comprathy.com**, and please use it if you find it useful to add to your vocabulary.

REFLECTION POINT 1.2

Think of a relationship in school that feels difficult.

- What might be the underlying fear?
- What's one step you could take this week to ease that fear?

COMMUNICATING CLEARLY UNDER PRESSURE

As a SENCo, you'll often have to deliver difficult messages – about limited funding, the reality of waiting lists, or why an EHCP isn't guaranteed. Clarity and honesty are your best tools. A few strategies I've found useful:

- **Stick to plain English**. Parents and teachers alike appreciate it when you translate acronyms and legal jargon.
- **Stay calm even if the other person is not**. Of course, you should not have to put up with verbal abuse, but as a professional, you need to remain professional and seek support during and after any negative interactions.
- **Be transparent**. If you don't know something, say so – and explain how you'll find out.
- **Use scripts**. Having a few 'set phrases' in your back pocket can reduce the pressure in heated situations. Example: Instead of saying 'We can't provide that,' try: 'Here's what we can do right now, and here's where we'll go next to explore further support.'

- **Facilitate whole school CPD for challenging conversations**. Supporting staff to develop the confidence and skills needed to communicate clearly, professionally, and compassionately with parents, colleagues, and external professionals.
- **Get the whole story for any in-class issues with students**. Get everyone's perspective before responding (even if the teacher involved is notorious for saying things that are not in line with best practice in SEND…). Having worked for a head who always shot first and asked questions later (always siding with the parent), I understand the frustrations.

For further support and ideas, including a sample school communication policy, see: **https://www.educationsupport.org.uk/resources/for-organisations/articles/partnering-with-parents-five-strategies-for-stronger-school-communities/**

INFLUENCING WITHOUT AUTHORITY

Many SENCos don't line-manage teachers, yet they are expected to shape classroom practice. Influence in this context comes less from formal authority and more from relationships and credibility.

Practical ways to influence:

- **Ask first.** Open the door to collaboration by asking 'What's working well for this student?'.
- **Model strategies.** If a teacher is unsure, offer to co-plan or co-teach.
- **Frame suggestions as shared problem solving.** Phrases like, 'Shall we try this together?' feel less threatening.

- **Support the IEP process.** Many teachers struggle with target setting and IEP paperwork; support them with training in this (don't do it for them though).
- **Secondary colleagues.** Consider how you can have a positive influence over a wider range of staff by creating small pockets of purposeful positive interaction that staff will remember and therefore try to embed.

Influence grows when staff feel you're on their side.

NAVIGATING DIFFICULT DYNAMICS AND STAYING GROUNDED

There will be times when you feel completely stuck in the middle – between staff and parents, between a child and a policy, or even between your own values and the system's demands. These moments are exhausting, but they're also part of the SENCo role.

The key is to separate what's in your control from what isn't. You can't fix the SEND Code of Practice overnight, but you can put structures in place in your school to make it more workable. You can't change the LA's waiting lists, but you can help a teacher adapt provision in the meantime.

Grounding strategies:

- Reflective journalling (a few lines each day about what's in/ out of your control). I use this cost-effective journal: https:// positiveyoungmind.com/product/journaling-for-senco-wellbeing/
- Peer support – sharing frustrations with other SENCos who 'get it.'
- Small wins – keeping a list of positive outcomes to balance the tough days.

REFLECTION POINT 1.3

Think about the parameters of your role.

- What are three things currently outside your control?
- How might you let go of them?
- What's one thing inside your control that you can act on this week?

ESTABLISHING STRONG LINKS WITH THE LOCAL AUTHORITY AND EXTERNAL PROFESSIONALS

No SENCo can work in isolation. Building relationships with the local authority and external professionals is crucial – not just to access provision, but to feel less isolated.

Tips:

- Be proactive: don't only contact the LA when you're sending negative gripes – send updates, share successes, and invite them into school. In my county, we have an Inclusion partner who is our first port of call and if you get assigned an effective one, a great LA relationship can be born (I appreciate that some LAs are more approachable and effective than others...)
- Build relationships with individual professionals (EPs, SALTs, OTs). A quick thank you email after a visit goes a long way.
- Network locally. SENCo clusters or forums can be a lifeline. As well as online forums such as mine (The Sweary SENCo Facebook Group), where SENCos' wellbeing is supported from

a realist perspective. If you get the chance, always attend face-to-face local cluster meetings; leaving site is always a breath of fresh air (literally). Try and organise at least one meeting a year in a coffee shop – and drop the guilt, because you've earned it.

The more connected you are, the less you'll feel like you're battling alone.

PULLING IT TOGETHER

Strong relationships don't happen overnight. They're built over time, through visibility, empathy, honesty, and persistence. But they're the foundation of everything else you'll do as a SENCo.

CLOSING THOUGHT

SENCoing is about people. You can have the best paperwork in the world, but without trust and strong relationships, nothing will change for students. With these elements as the keystone, even the biggest barriers can be overcome (or at least tackled with good humour and collaboration).

 NOTE IT DOWN

Create your own 'relationship map.' In one column, list your key stakeholders (leaders, teachers, LSAs, parents, LA, external professionals). In the next column, rate the current level of trust (high/medium/low RAG rate). In the final column, write one small action you could take this term to strengthen each relationship.

Remember: you don't need to transform every relationship at once. Aim for one positive amendment a week. Small, consistent actions, even if only marginal gains, build lasting influence.

CHAPTER 2

JUST GOOD TEACHING: A WHOLE-SCHOOL FOUNDATION FOR INCLUSION

This chapter will explore:

- How high-quality teaching forms the foundation of effective SEND support
- Why inclusion must be understood as a whole-school responsibility
- The differences between differentiation, adaptation, and scaffolding
- Practical, realistic approaches to reasonable adjustments across all phases

INTRODUCTION

If you ask teachers what makes the biggest difference to students with SEND, they will often mention interventions, 1:1 support, or specialist resources. These things matter – but the real cornerstone of inclusion is everyday classroom practice. 'Just good teaching' is the minimum expectation that all children should receive in school and with this phrase comes a significant amount of inclusion and adaptation as teaching cannot be good without it. It is about ensuring that every teacher, in every classroom, creates an environment where all students can access learning and succeed. That is not to say it isn't without its challenges. Even the most gifted teacher struggles at times with limited resources to cater for 30+ children, who have a wide and growing variety of needs.

For SENCos, this is both liberating and challenging. Liberating, because inclusion is not yours to carry alone: it belongs to the whole school (and you should have significant senior leader support when improving it). Challenging, because many staff still see SEND as something 'extra', a bolt-on responsibility that sits outside the core of their teaching. Part of your role is to shift this mindset.

This chapter explores what 'just good teaching' looks like in practice. It will give you ways to support staff in embedding inclusive strategies, show how to clarify common confusions, and offer quick wins that can transform the daily classroom experience. Above all, it reminds us that inclusion begins not with paperwork, but with pedagogy.

THE FIRST WAVE OF SUPPORT

'Just good teaching' is also known as 'high-quality teaching' (HQT) or called 'quality first teaching' (QFT) – I dislike both terms and would be the first in a staff meeting to inwardly roll my eyes when either was mentioned, especially when followed by a long list of non-negotiables… Whatever term your school uses, is still the first and most important layer of SEND support. Without it, interventions are wasted effort: if the classroom remains inaccessible, additional support can never compensate.

WHAT DOES GOOD, INCLUSIVE TEACHING LOOK LIKE?

Although every school has its own language and frameworks, there are some consistent features:

- **Clear, predictable routines**: students know what to expect and feel secure.
- **Explicit teaching of concepts**: teachers break down knowledge into manageable steps and model concepts well.
- **Active checking for understanding**: not just 'did you finish the task?' but 'can you explain what this means in your own words?'
- **Strategic use of scaffolds**: temporary supports such as writing frames or word banks that can be gradually removed (or not).
- **Purposeful use of visuals and dual coding**: diagrams, timelines, and symbols that anchor understanding.
- **Positive behaviour (SEMH) management**: proactive strategies that build on strengths, rather than reactive punishments such as safe spaces.

Why it matters

When good inclusive teaching is embedded:

- Students with SEND are less likely to be isolated or withdrawn from lessons.
- Teachers feel more confident, reducing dependency on the SENCo (this saves so much of your time).
- Families experience greater consistency and reassurance.

REFLECTION POINT 2.1

Think about your staff as a whole.

- Which are excellent at adaptation and inclusion?
- Are there any missing elements that need whole-school training?
- Do any of your staff need a mindset shift?

INCLUSION AS A COLLECTIVE RESPONSIBILITY

One of the (many) hard parts of being a SENCo is challenging the belief that inclusion is 'your job'. In reality, inclusion is everyone's job. Students with SEND spend the majority of their time in classrooms, unless there are significant and complex needs, and even then, we are working towards classrooms to be supportive of as many needs as possible for as long as possible. If the classroom environment does not have the foundations of inclusion, then catering for more complex needs becomes all the more difficult. This said, I also remember what it is like to try to teach a class with a diverse range of needs effectively – my lived experience of this helps me as a SENCo, as I am rarely surprised and have many tools and suggestions in my toolbox. Neither am I ashamed to admit that my early attempts at supporting children with SEND and SEMH needs (back in the days when inclusion as a concept wasn't so prevalent), a lot of my knowledge and understanding about what works and what doesn't, have largely been trial and error. With increasing needs in today's classrooms, teachers need to know what is proven to work quickly, thus whole school inclusive strategies are paramount.

Embedding collective responsibility

In order to achieve collective responsibility we must:

- **Set clear expectations:** Make 'inclusive teaching' part of the school's fabric.
- **Provide inductions for new staff:** Give every new colleague a guide to your school's SEND expectations, so they understand from day one.
- **Drip-feed CPD:** Instead of one-off SEND INSETs, use staff briefings to share bite-sized strategies. Teachers can try one thing at a time, building confidence gradually.
- **Celebrate good practice:** Share examples where inclusive strategies have worked well. Recognition encourages replication.

SHIFTING THE MINDSET

Colleagues may resist, saying 'I don't have time' or 'that's not my job'. From what I've seen in schools and my networks, this seems to be a particular issue in secondary schools with many more staff personalities in comparison to primary. After suggesting what a SENCo job is versus what a teacher's job is on one of my TikTok videos, a lot of unhappy teachers came back and said that school simply didn't give effective CPD or enough support in this area and this of course, is sometimes true. Schools, SENCos and teachers are walking a thin line to get the balance of staff support and staff expectations right. I have put together a handy table (Table 2.1) of what can be considered the SENCo role and the teacher's role, and where they overlap (this may of course differ in individual schools).

A useful response is to frame inclusion as *good teaching for everyone*. Many adjustments – breaking down tasks, using visuals, allowing processing time – benefit the whole class, not just those with SEND. Once these things are embedded effectively, staff can start to see the benefits themselves and they save time as a result.

Table 2.1   Understanding SENCo and teacher responsibilities

SENCo – strategic and statutory leadership	Shared responsibility – collaboration	Class teacher – day-to-day practice
Ensure statutory SEND duties are met	Work in partnership with clear communication	Deliver consistently strong tier-1 teaching
Provide guidance, support and CPD for staff	Identify needs and agree support actions together	Flag concerns and seek support early
Lead on LSA deployment and training	Discuss pupils, progress and next steps regularly	Deploy LSAs effectively within the classroom
Monitor SEND provision and progress at a strategic level	Use pupil progress meetings to inform decisions	Monitor individual pupil progress and outcomes
Coordinate referrals, assessments and EHCP processes	Jointly prepare referral and assessment paperwork	Contribute evidence for referrals and assessments
Collate and quality-assure IEPs	Co-produce high-quality, meaningful IEPs	Write and review IEPs based on classroom evidence

THE POWER OF EMPATHY

A very effective way of helping staff be mindful of individual needs is to allow them to actually experience a snapshot of what it is like for individual students. This could be achieved in a variety of ways, such as using the sensory bus which is a specially adapted vehicle designed to provide a calming, multi-sensory environment with features such as lights, sounds, textures (or your own version), to simulate what it is like for students with ASD or get access to wheelchairs for a staff meeting on physical impairment. As an increasingly busy society, I can see a downfall of empathy in every sector, not just education. We need to get this back. Pockets of this are improving all over the world. Here is a Japanese example where health practitioners are expected to train using an elderly simulation suit: https://www.youtube.com/shorts/o7UIOkwaOk8. Pre-2014 curriculum, I remember having many more quality interactions with students because I had more time to talk to them. I feel this has eroded with today's expectations and our empathy levels alongside it.

 **IDEAS FOR THE CLASSROOM 2.1**

Introduce a 'strategy of the month' across the school (but build on these by keeping the previous strategy). For example:

- January: Pre-teaching key vocabulary.
- February: Using mini-whiteboards to check for understanding.
- March: Providing dual coding (words + images).

Encourage staff to share at the end of each month:

- What impact did it have?
- What challenges came up?
- Will you keep using it?

DIFFERENTIATION, ADAPTATION, SCAFFOLDING AND PERSONALISATION

Teachers often use these terms interchangeably, but clarity is vital. Understanding the differences empowers staff to make confident decisions.

- **Differentiation** means planning different routes for students to achieve similar learning goal at levels appropriate for the individual. For example, one group might write an extended essay, while another produces a labelled diagram.
- **Adaptation** means adjusting how material is delivered while keeping the task and objective the same. For instance, a teacher might provide instructions verbally, visually, and in writing, so all students can access the task to achieve the same learning goal.
- **Scaffolding** means providing temporary supports to enable access. This could be sentence starters, word mats, or structured worksheets. The goal is to phase these out over time as independence grows.
- **Personalised Curriculum** is when a student is working significantly below ARE, so a more personalised curriculum – that works towards individual learning objectives – is needed. This will likely come from EHCP outcomes. The Engagement Model is appropriate here. This is also differentiation and needs a higher level of SENCo support to oversee provision.
- **Hybrid Inclusion Model** provides the best of whole-class inclusive teaching with elements of personalisation when appropriate. In reality, many students are working within a best-fit, in-between model. They are neither fully accessing the curriculum in the same way as their peers, nor operating on a completely personalised pathway. Their learning sits in the middle, shaped by need, support, and responsiveness.

For further information on these topics read my blog posts:

- https://positiveyoungmind.com/hybrid-inclusion-model/
- https://positiveyoungmind.com/adaption-scaffolding-differentiation/
- https://positiveyoungmind.com/personalisation-engagement-model/

WHY TEACHERS GET STUCK

Some teachers believe differentiation always means 'creating three versions of the worksheet'. This is unsustainable (although sometimes entirely appropriate). By showing the range of adaptations and scaffolds available, you help staff to realise they can be inclusive without doubling their workload. It should also be noted that adaptation should always happen at both the planning stage and the 'on-the-hop' whilst teaching stage. So often teachers have taken adaptation to mean 'differentiation by outcome' (i.e. none!) and then needed to adapt in the moment, often unsuccessfully.

 **REFLECTION POINT 2.2**

Spend some time shadowing a few individual students on your SEND list.

- Is their teacher differentiating, adapting, personalising or scaffolding?
- Which of those approaches best matches the student's needs right now?
- Is the strategy working for the student? Does it need to be more carefully thought out or more efficient?
- Are there any students who are clearly struggling in class and need more specialist intervention, curriculum or funding?

HINTS & TIPS 2.1

Quick reminders for staff:

- Scaffolds can be temporary: phase them out when students are ready (but reinstate if needed).
- Adaptations are sustainable: one change in delivery benefits many students – even non-SEND.
- Differentiation is sometimes needed, but not always: don't overcomplicate.
- These strategies need to be considered both whilst teaching and at the planning stage.
- For complex needs, a personalised curriculum (or hybrid model) may be more appropriate.

PRACTICAL APPROACHES TO REASONABLE ADJUSTMENTS

Reasonable adjustments can sound daunting, but they are often small, common-sense changes. What makes them powerful is consistency. Also, refer to the EEF's '5 a day' approach, which recommends five core practices (Aubin, 2022):

1. Explicit instruction
2. Cognitive and metacognitive strategies
3. Scaffolding
4. Flexible grouping
5. Using technology

You can read about this approach here: https://educationendowmentfoundation.org.uk/news/eef-blog-the-five-a-day-approach-how-the-eef-can-support

Examples from practice

- **Primary:** A Year 2 teacher uses a visual timetable and allows a child to check off activities. Anxiety reduces, behaviour improves, and learning time increases.
- **Secondary:** A science teacher provides students with a 'lab script' in advance, so they know the sequence of the experiment. Students with processing difficulties are more confident, and the whole class benefits.
- **EYFS:** A reception class teacher uses Now/Next boards. Students with SEND transition more smoothly, and peers pick up the routine too.

QUICK WINS FOR STAFF

- Give instructions in short steps and check understanding.
- Use seating strategically: near positive role models, away from distractions.
- Allow extra time for processing and responding.
- Provide word banks or sentence starters to support writing.
- Reinforce learning with visuals and gestures.

IDEAS FOR THE CLASSROOM 2.2

Create a 'reasonable adjustments menu' for staff.

- One side lists 10–15 strategies (e.g. visual prompts, extra time, chunked instructions).
- The other side invites staff to tick which ones they've tried.

Encourage teachers to select one new adjustment each fortnight and reflect on the outcome.

PULLING IT TOGETHER

'Just good teaching' is not about perfection or complexity. It is about consistent, inclusive practice across the whole school. When staff understand that inclusion is a shared responsibility, and when they are confident in small, practical strategies, students with SEND thrive.

For you as SENCo, the aim is to reduce firefighting and build a culture where staff know what to do first. Instead of always being the problem solver, you become the enabler – helping staff to embed good practice, share successes, and gradually shift the school culture.

NOTE IT DOWN

Create your own 'Inclusion Audit'.

- In one column, list the features of high-quality teaching (routines, scaffolds, visuals, checking for understanding, etc.).
- In the next column, rate each feature in your school (high/medium/low).
- In the final column, write one action you could take this term to strengthen consistency.

Top tip: Don't try to improve everything at once. Choose one feature, embed it, and move on. Small, steady shifts are more sustainable than one-off bursts of change.

For a full SEND self-review and tracking grid see: https://positive youngmind.com/product/sendreview/

CHAPTER 3
CONNECTION AND CONFIDENCE: LEADING AS A SENCO

This chapter will explore:

- How to make the transition from classroom teacher to SENCo
- Leading and managing support staff effectively
- Building confidence and credibility with colleagues and SLT
- Reducing isolation through networking and professional communities

INTRODUCTION

Stepping into the SENCo role can feel like moving into a new country without a map. Many teachers arrive here with little formal training, yet are immediately expected to manage staff, influence classroom practice, and represent SEND at leadership level. It is no wonder that confidence is often the first casualty.

The good news? Confidence grows through connection. Leading well as a SENCo isn't about having all the answers, it's about building relationships, learning on the job, and recognising that mistakes and owning that you don't know 'yet' are part of the process. This chapter explores how you can develop confidence in yourself while also helping others feel confident in you.

FROM CLASSROOM TEACHER TO SENCO

The shift from class teacher to SENCo is significant. As a teacher, success is measured by what happens in your classroom. As a SENCo, your impact is indirect: you support others so that students succeed in many classrooms.

Challenges in transition

- **Loss of immediacy:** You no longer see the direct progress of a single class.
- **New responsibilities:** You suddenly manage processes like EHCPs, referrals, and statutory deadlines.
- **Knowledge:** Colleagues may expect you to know every answer instantly.
- **Authority without power:** You influence teaching without directly line-managing most teachers and sometimes not having much say (or even a voice) in how your school is run.

Reframing the role

Instead of measuring success by what you do, measure it by what others can do because of your support. If a teacher adapts their practice after your input, that's impact. If an LSA feels valued and motivated, that's leadership.

REFLECTION POINT 3.1

Think back to your first year in the SENCo role (or imagine it if you are brand new).

- What surprised you most about the shift?
- Which part of your teacher identity has helped you?
- Which part have you had to let go of?
- How have you reframed your place in your school or adapted to a new school?

LEADING AND MANAGING SUPPORT STAFF

Support staff are often the unsung heroes of SEND provision. They work most closely with students who need the most help, yet they may receive the least training and recognition. Your role in leading them is crucial.

Principles for managing LSAs and TAs

- **Clarity of role:** Ensure support staff understand their purpose in each lesson. Are they promoting independence, scaffolding, or managing behaviour?

- **Regular communication:** Hold short but regular catch-ups. Five minutes of clarity saves hours of confusion.
- **Professional respect:** Involve support staff in discussions about students. They hold valuable insights and often have better relationships with individual students than class teachers do.
- **Training and CPD:** Even small, informal sessions build confidence and skill.

When things are tricky

It's not unusual for support staff to feel undervalued or frustrated. Sometimes they are pulled in different directions by teachers, leaders, and parents. A key part of your leadership is to advocate for them, ensuring they have consistent expectations and support, especially if you directly line manage them.

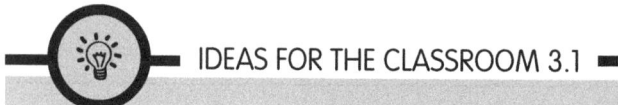 **IDEAS FOR THE CLASSROOM 3.1**

Run a short 'role clarity' activity with support staff:

- Ask them to list what they believe their role is during lessons.
- Compare it with what teachers think their role is.
- Discuss overlaps and differences, then agree on shared expectations.

This simple exercise reduces confusion and raises professional confidence.

The EEF's advice on making the best use of teaching assistants, which can be read here: https://eef.dev/education-evidence/guidance-reports/teaching-assistants, (although I only agree with 95% of it), is a great resource to plan training and provide clarity to the role.

BUILDING CONFIDENCE WITH COLLEAGUES AND SLT

Confidence as a SENCo is partly about how you see yourself, but it is also about how others perceive you. Credibility matters. Staff need to know that you are approachable, knowledgeable, and reliable.

Practical ways to build credibility

- **Be visible:** Drop into classrooms regularly, not just when there are problems.
- **Communicate clearly:** Use plain English and avoid overwhelming staff with acronyms.
- **Admit what you don't know:** Colleagues respect honesty. Say, 'I'll find out and get back to you.'
- **Share small wins:** Highlight positive outcomes in staff meetings to show SEND progress is possible.

Working with SLT

You may or may not sit on the senior leadership team. Either way, you need to influence decisions at that level, as stated in the 2025 OFSTED framework.

- Provide evidence: data, case studies, or student voice that demonstrate impact.

- Link SEND priorities to whole-school goals (attendance, attainment, wellbeing).
- Show solutions, not just problems. Leaders respond better to 'Here's the issue and here's one way we might address it' than to 'This is a problem and I'm stuck.'

The SENCo being a part of SLT issue remains ambiguous. For more on this see: https://positiveyoungmind.com/senco-slt/

REFLECTION POINT 3.2

Consider your current relationship with SLT. RAG rate your ability to influence these areas effectively:

- Positioning and role clarity: SENCo as part of SLT with statutory responsibilities and time for leadership.
- Strategic voice in decision-making: influence over improvement planning, budgets, curriculum, and data use.
- Advocacy for inclusion: championing student and family voice, embedding SEND in safeguarding and wellbeing.
- Relational influence: building trust, acting as a bridge, and mentoring colleagues to strengthen practice.
- Operational leadership: leading provision mapping, budgets, and monitoring impact for SLT and governors.
- Cultural influence: modelling inclusive leadership, embedding staff wellbeing, and promoting equity.
- External leverage: using networks, ensuring inspection readiness, and raising the school's profile.

Consider which areas are not effective and discuss with your school leaders

HINTS & TIPS 3.1

- Quick updates keep SLT aware without adding to meeting agendas – create a shared document you can all annotate.
- Keep a one-page 'SEND snapshot' to share with leaders every two weeks: headline data, priorities, and success stories.
- Consider how you can positively influence at leadership level if you don't have a seat at the table – use the OFSTED framework as an incentive.
- Raise your profile in school: see: https://positiveyoungmind.com/sencos-raising-the-profile-of-these-unsung-heros/

REDUCING ISOLATION THROUGH NETWORKING

SENCoing can feel lonely. In many schools, you are the only person in the role. Yet connection with others is one of the fastest ways to reduce stress and build confidence.

Local networks

- **Cluster meetings:** Many local authorities run SENCo clusters. These can be invaluable for sharing strategies and feeling less alone.
- **School partnerships:** Reach out to neighbouring schools to compare practice.

Online communities

- **Specialist forums and groups:** There are active SENCo networks on social media such as my wellbeing Facebook group, 'The Sweary SENCo': https://www.facebook.com/groups/theswearysenco/
- **Professional organisations:** NASEN, EEF and others provide resources and webinars.

Benefits of networking

- Shared understanding: others 'get it' without explanation.
- Practical solutions: what has worked elsewhere may work for you.
- Emotional support: knowing you're not the only one facing the challenge.

SOS – for when it gets too much

- I have an emergency SOS button on my website: https://positiveyoungmind.com/senco-resources/ or you can utilise The Sweary SENCO Facebook group for ideas and solidarity.
- Contact Ed Support at https://www.educationsupport.org.uk/

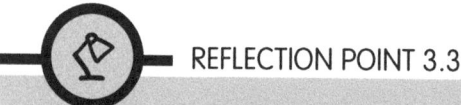

REFLECTION POINT 3.3

What networks are currently available to you?

- Local authority clusters
- Online communities
- Professional associations

Which of these could you commit to engaging with more regularly this week, this term and this year?

 IDEAS FOR THE CLASSROOM 3.2

Organise a 'SEND roundtable' with colleagues from nearby schools.

- Bring one success story and one challenge each.
- Share strategies and resources.
- Leave with at least one new idea to try in your own setting.

It doesn't need to be formal. Meeting in a coffee shop can make it more relaxed and sustainable. Do this unapologetically and without guilt – just don't mention names as walls have ears!

PULLING IT TOGETHER

Confidence as a SENCo grows through practice, relationships, and persistence. No one enters the role fully prepared. What matters is a willingness to learn, a commitment to connection, and a recognition that leadership is about influence rather than authority.By leading support staff well, building credibility with colleagues and SLT, and engaging with networks beyond your school, you create a foundation not only for your own confidence but for a stronger SEND culture across your setting.

NOTE IT DOWN

Create your own 'confidence map'.

- In one column, list the groups you interact with (teachers, LSAs, SLT, parents, external professionals).
- In the next column, rate your current confidence with each group (high/medium/low).
- In the final column, write one small step you could take this term to increase your confidence with that group.

Small actions like clarifying a role, joining a cluster meeting, or preparing a one-page briefing, build long-term confidence and credibility.

CHAPTER 4
NAVIGATING STATUTORY DUTIES WITH CONFIDENCE

This chapter will explore an overview of:

- Understanding the SENCo's statutory responsibilities and where they overlap with teaching staff
- Making sense of the SEND Code of Practice
- Handling EHCPs and key paperwork effectively
- Future-proofing your knowledge through trusted sources and systems

INTRODUCTION

One of the first things SENCos often say is, 'I don't know enough about the law.' Statutory duties can feel overwhelming, especially when acronyms multiply and deadlines pile up. Let me assure you that you don't need to know every clause of every policy. But what you do need is a clear understanding of your responsibilities, reliable sources of information, and systems that make compliance sustainable – especially when attempting to extract money out of your local authority! This chapter is designed to take some of the pain out of statutory duties. Rather than a checklist of every piece of legislation, it will focus on the essentials: what you as a SENCo must know (or at least be familiar with and able to find at short notice), what others should be doing, and how to stay informed.

THE SENCO'S CORE RESPONSIBILITIES

Every SENCo should be familiar with (mainly section 6) of the SEND Code of Practice (2015), but that does not mean memorising it – It's not exactly bedtime reading! At its heart, the SENCo role includes:

- Overseeing the day-to-day operation of the school's SEND policy
- Coordinating provision for children with SEND
- Advising on the graduated approach to providing support
- Working with parents and external agencies
- Maintaining records and ensuring statutory deadlines are met
- Reporting to governors and SLT on SEND provision

Who does what?

One of the biggest pitfalls is taking on work that belongs elsewhere. For example:

- **Teachers** remain responsible for the progress of all students in their class, including those with SEND.
- **Support staff** implement strategies but should not be left to plan provision without oversight.
- **The SENCo** coordinates, advises, and quality assures – not single-handedly delivers.

Clarifying these roles early (with SLT as well), prevents the 'all SEND is yours' problem that leaves SENCos buried in tasks.

Please refer to Table 2.1, which highlights roles and responsibilities.

REFLECTION POINT 4.1

Think about your current workload.

- Are you doing tasks that should belong to class teachers?
- Where might you need to push back or reframe responsibility?
- How clear are staff in your school about who does what?
- Do your school leaders also have a good understanding of which responsibilities belong to who?

MAKING SENSE OF THE SEND CODE OF PRACTICE

The Code of Practice is over 250 pages long, but not every page is relevant to daily SENCo work. I would recommend printing at least section 6 out.

The key sections for most practitioners are:

- The graduated approach (Assess, Plan, Do, Review)
- The responsibilities of class teachers
- Statutory timescales for EHCP processes
- The emphasis on co-production with families

Your job is not to be a walking encyclopaedia but to know where to find the answer and how to apply it. It is especially helpful to be able quote useful parts of the Code of Practice. Another helpful tool in your toolkit to enable you to use the document effectively is to employ the help of the GPT I designed especially for SENCos. 'Ask Sarah Swail' (because 'Swail' is a cross between swear and wail…), is invaluable for this purpose. Give her a try on anything from legislation to SENCo wellbeing: https://chatgpt.com/g/g-689a5483b7ec8191804f3712c413fc2e-ask-sarah-swail

It is also worth remembering that The Code of Practice **DOES NOT** trump the law so if your local authority is using it to ask you to do something, always check with the Children and Families Act.

The law that trumps the SEND Code of Practice is the Children and Families Act 2014.

The Code of Practice provides statutory guidance, which means schools and local authorities must have regard to it, but it does not override the law itself. The Act, along with associated regulations such as the Special Educational Needs and Disability Regulations 2014 and the Equality Act 2010, forms the legal foundation for SEND provision.

So, in short:

- Children and Families Act 2014 = Primary legislation (the 'law').
- SEND Regulations 2014 = Secondary legislation (sets out how the law is implemented).

- SEND Code of Practice (2015) = Statutory guidance (explains how to apply the law in practice).

If there's ever a conflict, the Act and Regulations take precedence over the Code. A simple way to remember it is Law > Regulations > Code of Practice > Local Policy (see Figure 4.1).

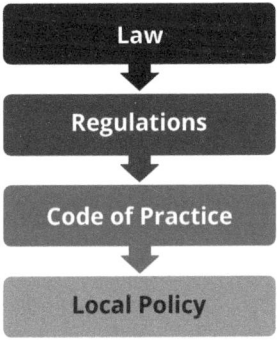

Figure 4.1   The hierarchy of guidance

PRACTICAL STRATEGIES

- Keep a bookmarked digital copy of the Code for quick searches or employ AI.
- Highlight or summarise the sections most relevant to your phase (e.g. early years, primary, secondary).
- Create one-page crib sheets for staff: 'What teachers need to know about the Code.'
- Use professional organisations (NASEN, Whole School SEND) for updated summaries and resources.

HINTS & TIPS 4.1

- Don't reinvent the wheel: use existing guidance from trusted organisations.
- Share updates in small doses: one slide in a staff briefing is more effective than an hour-long lecture.
- Translate legal jargon into plain English: 'This is what the Code says,' followed by 'This is what it means for you in your classroom.'

EHCPS AND THE LEGAL FRAMEWORK

Few areas of the SENCo role cause more stress than Education, Health and Care Plans (EHCPs). The process can feel daunting, with strict timelines, complex paperwork, and high expectations from families. Confidence grows when you understand the sequence, know what to do when things don't go to plan, and have systems in place to keep everything on track.

In schools with high needs it is worth sitting down with your line manager or head to discuss the order of priority for EHC Needs Assessment (EHCNA) applications before you even apply. This will support parental conversations. When you have ten students who need an EHCP, it is tricky to have conversations with parents whose child is not the highest priority for your school – and if the decision has been made jointly, it is much easier. It is also worth taking into account which parents would be able to apply themselves. Let them know the process would be faster overall if they do this, especially in situations where parents have the skills to be able to navigate the system or when the school deems that the need for the student to have an EHCP is incredibly low. This leaves you more opportunity to support students whose parents do not have the skills in this area and cannot navigate the complexities of getting an EHCP. Even when parents have applied themselves, I've always offered to proofread and suggest a few extra points to add in if needed. It is both a challenging and depressing system, but *schools should not be the gatekeepers for students to access an EHCNA*.

If the student meets the legal threshold, then parents and schools are entitled to apply.

APPLYING FOR AN EHC NEEDS ASSESSMENT (EHCNA)

Anyone can request an EHC needs assessment – including parents, carers, or the school – but schools are usually expected to provide clear evidence that they have already followed a *graduated response*. This means showing what has been tried, what impact it has had, and why further support is needed. A note here is that your APDR process does not have to be one IEP per term; you can shorten the timeframe to every few weeks if you wish, especially if the need is urgent and the provision is increasing. In no time, you'll have three APDR cycles.

It should also be noted that legally, you only need to provide a letter that takes less than an hour to write and does not need to be on your LA's form. IPSEA provide model letters to use. This is because the legal threshold is as follows.

Children and Families Act 2014, Section 36(8):

'The local authority must secure an EHC needs assessment for the child or young person if, *having considered the evidence*, it is of the opinion that:

(a) the child or young person *may have special educational needs*, and (b) *it may be necessary* for special educational provision to be made for the child or young person in accordance with an EHC plan.'

This is known as the 'two-part test' and it sets a deliberately low threshold. The key words are *'may have'* and *'may be necessary'*. It does not say 'must have', 'definitely has', or 'after all school resources are exhausted'. Use this to your advantage.

This issue is notoriously challenging for SENCos and schools, as although you technically only have to provide a letter outlining needs, for your LA to notice your EHCNA in a tsunami of other EHCNAs they are receiving, it is worth making it stand out, especially as you will need to provide more evidence further down the line anyway. My webinars, 'Writing an EHCNA That Gets Noticed!' (https://positiveyoungmind.com/product/%f0%9f%a6%9a-writing-an-ehcna/) and 'Challenge Your LA' (https://positiveyoungmind.com/product/challenge-your-la/) have been hugely popular as a result of these challenges.

When parents and schools disagree about an EHCNA

Sometimes, parents and schools don't share the same view about whether an Education, Health and Care needs assessment (EHCNA) is needed. These situations can feel uncomfortable, but the law is clear:

- **If parents want to apply and the school does not agree:** Parents (or the young person, if over 16) have an *independent right* to request an EHC needs assessment under Section 36(1) of the *Children and Families Act 2014*. They do not need the school's permission. The local authority must then consider the request and apply the two-part legal test in Section 36(8) – whether the child *may have* SEN and *may need* provision via an EHCP. The LA cannot refuse to assess simply because the school didn't make the request.

- **If the school believes an EHCNA is needed but parents
  do not agree:** The school can still make a request, but should
  inform parents and ideally seek consent. The law allows the
  LA to proceed without parental consent if it considers an
  assessment necessary, under Section 36(3). However, it is
  unlikely that the LA will wish to proceed in these circumstances.
  Also, best practice is to maintain open communication and
  reassure parents that the purpose of the assessment is to
  identify needs, not to label or make irreversible decisions.

In both scenarios, it helps to:

- Meet with the parent(s) to explain what an assessment involves
  and what it does not mean.
- Focus on shared aims – improving understanding of need and
  securing appropriate support.
- Keep notes of discussions and decisions, in case the LA later
  asks for evidence of parental involvement.

Key steps

- Request to assess: Send your EHCNA request to the local
  authority (LA). Include clear evidence of needs, interventions,
  progress data, and professional input.
- LA decision: The LA must respond within six weeks, deciding
  whether to assess.
- Assessment phase: If agreed, professionals (EPs, SALTs, OTs,
  etc.) contribute reports, usually within six weeks.
- Draft plan: The LA produces a draft EHCP based on the
  evidence.
- Final plan: The plan should be issued within 20 weeks of the
  original request.

If the LA refuses to assess or issue a plan

- Ask for the reasons in writing.
- Meet with your SEN Case Officer to discuss next steps.
- Parents (and schools, with parental consent) have the right to appeal to the SEND Tribunal.
- While awaiting appeal, continue to gather evidence and maintain support through SEN Support.
- If there is new or further evidence, a new request can be made at any time.

Delays can happen due to missed reports, changes in personnel, or LA capacity issues. Keep a timeline tracker and regularly check in with professionals. If deadlines are missed, it's appropriate to remind the LA of their statutory duty to complete the process within 20 weeks. Parents have slightly more legal weight so any complaints, mediations, tribunal and ombudsman escalations coming from them are also helpful.

In the current educational climate, it is a long road, even for the most complex of SEND needs. It requires persistence, tenacity and downright bloody mindedness to achieve the outcome that is best for the child at times. Make a polite nuisance of yourself as much as possible and ensure your school leaders and governors are backing you up.

Recent commentary suggests that Local Authorities' win rate is extremely low – one report states that in 2023-24 only 150 out of 11,157 appeals were upheld in full, giving an LA 'success rate' of ~1.3 % (Keer, 2024).

WHEN THE PLAN IS IN PLACE

Once an EHCP is issued, it becomes a *legally binding document*. The school must deliver everything written in Section F (Special Educational Provision). It's important to note that:

- Section F is written by the LA, not the school.
- SENCos and schools can suggest amendments or request clarification, but the LA holds responsibility for final wording and changes.
- If provision is unclear, request a written explanation from the LA before signing off the draft.

Transparency is key. Using a costed provision map helps everyone understand where funding is allocated and what additional provision is in place. This supports accountability and makes discussions with parents clearer, especially where resources are stretched. ALWAYS request further funding when there is a shortfall between section F provision needs and funding and keep badgering until you get what you require.

Reviewing and Amending the EHCP

The EHCP must be reviewed at least annually, but an early or interim review can be called if needs change significantly.

Reasons to request an early review:

- The child's needs have increased or changed.
- The current provision is not sufficient.
- You are requesting a change in funding banding or type of setting.

At annual review:

- Ensure progress towards EHCP outcomes is discussed.
- Discuss updates to school-based IEPs or support plans so that short-term targets link clearly to EHCP outcomes – I like to set yearly targets for this reason, which makes it easier to link between the EHCP outcomes and termly IEPS.

- Document any requests for change in provision or funding, and ensure this is captured in the review paperwork sent back to the LA.

If the LA does not agree to amend the plan despite clear evidence, you can:

- Request a reconsideration in writing.
- Escalate through LA complaints or, with parental consent, support the family to appeal to Tribunal.

Keeping everyone on the same page

- Share the latest version of the EHCP with all relevant staff.
- Break down Section F into actionable steps on IEPs, student profiles and/or provision maps.
- Keep parents informed using straightforward language – explain what the plan includes, what the school is responsible for, and where to go if they have questions.

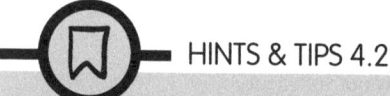 **HINTS & TIPS 4.2**

My website offers free downloadable SENCo resources, including template documents for setting out individual provision plans, these can be found here https://positiveyoungmind.com/senco-resources/

Using these:

- Create a provision map for each student with an EHCP.
- Create your own section F provision evaluation document for each student with an EHCP.

IDEAS FOR THE CLASSROOM 4.1

Support teachers with translating EHCP outcomes into the classroom.

- Ensure they understand that the EHCP outcomes are what they are aiming for by the end of key stage.
- It's important to be aspirational but also realistic with targets.
- RAG rate section F to see how well the school is meeting statutory duties for your student (using the Excel grid available on my website or similar).
- Ensure transparency: work together to identify gaps in provision, funding mismatches and unsuitable targets. Alert the local authority to request a review.

REFLECTION POINT 4.2

Consider your students with EHCPs

- Do you know how well section F is being implemented for each student?
- Are there costed provision maps in place to aid transparency for each student?
- Are parents aware of any shortfalls between section F and reality in school?
- Are any issues in meeting section F school based or LA based or a mixture?
- How will any issues be addressed?

FUTUREPROOFING YOUR KNOWLEDGE

Legislation and guidance change. What is true this year may shift with a new Code, government policy, or local authority protocol. Instead of memorising every detail, build habits that keep you up to date.

Where to look

- **Government websites:** Official updates on statutory guidance.
- **Professional organisations:** NASEN, Whole School SEND, and Education Endowment Foundation.
- **Peer networks:** Local clusters often share updates promptly.
- **Social media:** Follow credible SEND professionals, but always double-check sources.

Building systems

- Schedule time once a term to review updates.
- Keep a 'statutory duties' tracker with key deadlines and responsibilities.
- Share updates with SLT so they recognise the importance of SEND compliance.
- Train colleagues to take ownership of paperwork, so the responsibility does not fall entirely on you.

IDEAS FOR THE CLASSROOM 4.2

Create a list of statutory duties for your setting and develop a traffic light system.

- Green: systems are in place and working well (e.g. annual reviews completed on time).

- Amber: needs attention (e.g. some staff not completing paperwork promptly).
- Red: urgent (e.g. a deadline at risk of being missed).

Review the system with SLT each term. This makes SEND duties visible and keeps leaders accountable.

REFLECTION POINT 4.3

Think about how confident you feel in your current knowledge of statutory duties.

- Which areas feel clear and manageable?
- Where do you feel uncertain or out of date?
- What steps could you take this term to strengthen your confidence?

PULLING IT TOGETHER

By clarifying roles, simplifying the Code of Practice, managing EHCP processes with efficient systems, and future-proofing your knowledge, you can handle the legal side of the SENCo role with confidence. The aim is not to know everything but to know enough, and to build structures that protect you and your students. Talk them over with your head teacher or line manager so that it is not only you making decisions. Joined up thinking and collaboration is key.

 NOTE IT DOWN

Create your own statutory duties checklist:

- In one column, list your core responsibilities (SEND policy, EHCP timelines, annual reviews, governor reports).
- In the next column, identify what system you already have in place.
- In the final column, mark one action that would make each system more efficient.

By breaking down the legal load into manageable chunks, you will feel more in control and less at risk of missing key duties.

CHAPTER 5
SUSTAINING YOURSELF IN THE ROLE: SELF-CARE AND ORGANISATIONAL STRATEGIES

This chapter will explore:

- Recognising the emotional demands of the SENCo role
- Practical strategies for organisation and working smartly
- Protecting your wellbeing through boundaries and self-care
- Knowing when to seek help or consider a change of setting

INTRODUCTION

The SENCo role is rewarding but demanding. It carries responsibility for some of the most vulnerable children in the school, as well as for the colleagues who support them. SENCos often describe feeling pulled in every direction: from statutory deadlines and leadership demands to teachers seeking advice and parents needing reassurance. Add to this the emotional weight of listening to families' struggles, managing distressed students, and navigating systemic frustrations, and it becomes clear why burnout (and in some cases, plain exploitation), is common.

This chapter focuses on how to sustain yourself in the role with realistic organisational strategies, clear boundaries, and honest reflection on whether your setting is helping or harming your wellbeing.

THE EMOTIONAL DEMANDS OF THE SENCO ROLE

SENCos frequently encounter second-hand trauma, sometimes called compassion fatigue. Hearing about student and family experiences of neglect, abuse, or medical difficulties can take a toll. At the same time, you may be carrying guilt about not being able to 'fix' everything, as so much is outside of your control.

Common emotional pressures

- Supporting families in crisis while juggling statutory deadlines.
- Managing parental anger or distress, especially when resources are limited.
- Feeling responsible for staff wellbeing in addition to student progress.
- Balancing empathy with professional detachment.

Recognising these pressures is the first step. You are human and the system is broken. SENCos are increasingly being asked to do more with less time.

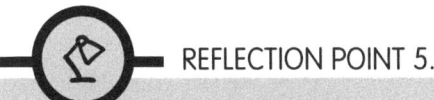

REFLECTION POINT 5.1

Think about the past half-term.

- Which situations have taken the biggest emotional toll on you?
- How did you respond at the time?
- Looking back, what could have helped you manage the impact more effectively?

ORGANISATIONAL STRATEGIES: WORKING SMARTLY

Organisation is one of the SENCo's greatest survival tools. Without clear systems, it is easy to feel like you are constantly firefighting.

Practical organisational tips

- **Prioritise:** Keep a running list, but identify your top three non-negotiables each day.
- **Batch tasks:** Group similar activities together (e.g. respond to all emails at once).
- **Use templates:** Save time by creating proformas for common tasks such as staff updates or parent letters.
- **Delegate:** Teachers should complete student passports or initial concern forms. Your role is to review, not to rewrite.
- **Plan protected time:** Block out diary slots for statutory paperwork or annual reviews and communicate to staff that these are non-negotiable.

Where you do not have time to complete all of your tasks, try this workload tracker to aid discussions with your school leaders (Table 5.1). Many have no idea of the hidden tasks of SENCoing that take up so much of your time. A version can be downloaded from: https://positiveyoungmind.com/senco-overview-of-workload-editable/

Table 5.1 SENCo workload tracker

Weekly	Phone calls / emails to outside agencies, e.g. NHS.
	Liaison with parents of concern pupils or pupils on register.
	Liaison with speech therapists.
	Learning walks to observe classes / SEND / concern pupils.
	Support for class teachers / LSAs etc.
	Reports and referrals for outside agencies such as NHS.
	SLT meeting and staff meeting.
	Catch-up meeting with safeguarding / behaviour lead.
	Monitoring of data.
	Monitoring and planning of interventions
	Monitoring – general SEND provision according to one plans.
	Update SEND register and distribute.
	Filing and report copying / distribution.
	SEND intervention groups and 1:1 and LAC pupil interventions.
	Gate duty / playground duty.

Fortnightly	Provision mapping target reviews.
	Monitoring of planning across year groups for SEND.
	Monitoring e.g. provision in class, progress – book looks.
	HT and SENCo catch up.
	Monitoring of intervention folders.
	Monitoring of one plan / provision map annotations.
Half-termly	Training for staff, ECTs etc.
	SEND parent coffee morning.
	Network meetings with Cluster and MAT.
	Gather info for and attend pupil progress meetings.
	Trustee / governor reports.
	Write and review SEND action plan.
	Review any children on the engagement model.
Termly	Parents evening attendance.
	Adjust health care plans as needed.
	Termly meeting with LA link (inclusion partner).
	Baseline assessments and repeat assessments (YARC etc.)
	Reviewing and collating one-page profiles.
	One plan meeting and collating one plans.
	Check website for updates needed.
	Check overview of progress and flag up any concerns.
	Termly visits and actions from specialist teachers / OTs etc.
	Review provision maps.
	LAC pupil monitoring and paperwork.
	Checking provision of EHCP pupils against EHCP statements.

(Continued)

Table 5.1   (Continued)

Annually	Transition for children going to and from setting.
	Attend needs assessment outcome meetings.
	Supporting parents with transitions, school choices.
	SEDAL / Boxall Assessments
	Apply for IPRA (health funding).
	Assess arrangements and assessments for these e.g. SATS.
	School development planning.
Ad Hoc	Attend team around the family meetings.
	Annual reviews and follow-up paperwork.
	Apply for EHCP needs assessments (8 hours+ per doc).
	Assess new starters and pupils of concern.
	Order SEND equipment.
	Class cover.
	General day-to-day issues.

 **IDEAS FOR THE CLASSROOM 5.1**

Create a SENCo concern form system (as if you are like me, you have no memory for quick corridor chats and things regularly fall off your inbox).

- Teachers complete a simple one-page form when worried about a student.
- This ensures concerns are documented and evidence is gathered.

- They need to write on it what QFT/tier-1 strategies they have tried.
- It also helps staff reflect before passing issues on, reducing unnecessary workload for you.
- Download a sample document here: https://positiveyoung mind.com/senco-resources/

Digital tools

- Use shared drives to store provision maps and paperwork.
- Explore calendar reminders for annual reviews and deadlines – set all annual review dates in September.
- Consider simple project management apps for tracking tasks and AI (following school GPDR), to reduce as much workload as you can.
- My AI 'Ask Sarah Swail' (see Chapter 4), has proven to be very helpful with lots of SENCos in my networks – she is certainly a realist (because that's how I programmed her!): https://chatgpt. com/g/g-689a5483b7ec8191804f3712c413fc2e-ask-sarah-swail

Organisation is not about doing everything; it is about ensuring that the right things get done.

REFLECTION POINT 5.2

Think about your confidence levels in your current systems.

- Which areas of your workload feel most chaotic?

(Continued)

- Which processes could be streamlined with a template, checklist, or shared resource?
- What is one system you could introduce this term to make life easier?

BOUNDARIES AND SELF-CARE

One of the hardest lessons for any SENCo is that there will always be more to do. Without boundaries, work expands to fill evenings, weekends and school holidays. Protecting your wellbeing is not selfish; it is essential to being effective in the role.

We should all be more selfish. If we keep ourselves happy, we have *more* ability to support others, not less.

Setting boundaries

- Decide when your working day ends – and stick to it.
- Use an out-of-office message during holidays to set clear expectations (especially for those pesky consultations the LA likes to sneak in).
- Learn to say 'no' to tasks that are not your responsibility.
- Use the phrase, 'I can help by...' to redirect tasks appropriately.

Self-care strategies

Self-care looks different for everyone. For some, it is physical activity; for others, it is reading, creative hobbies, or time with friends. The key is to make self-care non-negotiable. Ten minutes of daily journaling or a short walk can have as much impact as bigger interventions.

This includes during the school day. A 10-minute 'do not disturb' sign on the door for a quick round of breathing exercises or a lunchtime walk around the block for a change of scene all adds up.

HINTS & TIPS 5.1

- Build small wellbeing habits into your day, such as drinking water regularly or leaving your desk for lunch.
- Protect your evenings for non-work activities.
- Pair up with a colleague for mutual accountability: check in on each other's boundaries.
- Make yourself a wellbeing non-negotiable checklist and stick it on your desk.

REFLECTION POINT 5.3

Think about the boundaries you have currently.

- Which ones are working well?
- Where do you notice 'creep' – work taking over personal time?
- What one new boundary could you try this term?

WHEN THE SETTING ISN'T RIGHT

Sometimes the challenge is not just the workload but the culture of the school itself. A toxic environment – where SEND is undervalued, or SENCos are undermined – can damage wellbeing regardless of personal strategies. So many awesome SENCos in my networks report so little SENCo release time for their case loads, it's no wonder they are struggling.

Signs the culture may be harmful

- Leaders dismiss SEND concerns or refuse to allocate resources.
- Staff regularly undermine agreed strategies.
- You are excluded from leadership discussions that directly affect SEND provision.
- You feel constantly blamed rather than supported.

In these cases, the solution may be bigger than boundary-setting. It may involve seeking support from unions, governors, or external networks – or even considering a change of role or setting.

 **REFLECTION POINT 5.4**

Think about your current school environment.

- Does it support your wellbeing as a SENCo?
- Are there cultural barriers that make the role harder than it should be?
- What steps could you take if the setting is no longer healthy for you?
- Use this blog to help your reflection process: https://positiveyoungmind.com/toxic-schools-10-key-indicators-to-aid-workplace-reflection/

SEEKING HELP AND SUPPORT

SENCos often put themselves last on the list for support. Yet modelling help-seeking is powerful. It shows staff that wellbeing is a collective priority.

Sources of support

- **Peer networks:** Local SENCo clusters and online forums (such as The Sweary SENCo!)
- **Line managers:** Honest conversations about workload and priorities.
- **Professional organisations:** Education Support provides free helplines and resources.
- **Friends and family:** Sometimes you need a non-education perspective to reframe challenges.

 IDEAS FOR THE CLASSROOM 5.2

Build strong relationships with colleagues.

- Find time to find out about your colleagues' families and hobbies.
- When SENCoing feels isolating it is important to make the effort to build relationships.
- When those colleague relationships are strong, staff will be more willing to stick to deadlines and take into account your views.
- By doing this, you are building your support network in school. Remind colleagues of the breadth of your role.
- More profile-raising ideas here: https://positive youngmind.com/sencos-raising-the-profile-of-these-unsung-heros/

PULLING IT TOGETHER

Sustaining yourself as a SENCo requires a combination of emotional awareness, organisational systems, strong boundaries, and supportive networks. The role will always be demanding, but it does not need to be unsustainable. By recognising your limits, protecting your wellbeing, and creating efficient structures, you not only survive in the role but create the conditions to thrive. Remember: you cannot pour from an empty cup. Looking after yourself is the first step to looking after everyone else. With this in mind, having a strong support network outside of school is also important. I have needed to make a big effort to create this for myself as a single parent with a small family network.

Ultimately, it's just a job; your job shouldn't be your everything, it should be secondary to your actual life.

I have written extensively on the difficulties our profession faces at the moment and I am committed to making positive changes for all of us. Please refer to the following articles to find out more about my views on how much protected time you should get, your seat at the SLT table, holidays without interruption and fair pay.

- SENCo Pay: Clearing Up Confusion & Setting Out Fair Standards (https://positiveyoungmind.com/senco-pay/)
- SENCos and SLT: Clarity Needed (https://positiveyoungmind.com/senco-slt/)
- School Holiday Workload: Why SENCos Need Protection (https://positiveyoungmind.com/senco-protect-holiday/)
- SENCo Support: 5 Years On – Urgent Call for Protected Time (https://positiveyoungmind.com/protected-time/)

Here is my simplified proposal for *minimum* amounts of protected release time *per week* and support five years on from the original Bath Spa SENCo Wellbeing report (Table 5.2):

Table 5.2 Suggested minimum amounts of protected release time per week

Number of children on SEND register	Amount of protected SENCo time and support required (assistant time in brackets)	Number of children with an EHCP	Amount of extra SENCo protected time in addition to the second column
10	1 day	5	No extra time
20	2 days	5-10	0.5 days
30	3 days	10-15	1 day
40	4 days	15-20	1.5 days
50	5 days	20-25	2 days
60	5 days (+ 1 day)	25-30	2.5 days
70	5 days (+ 2 days)	30-35	3 days
80	5 days (+ 3 days)	35-40	3.5 days
90	5 days (+ 4 days)	40-50	4 days
100	5 days (+ 5 days)	45-50	4.5 days

Notes

For larger numbers of children on the SEND register, the pattern can be continued in the same increments.

For caseloads of more than 100, more than one qualified SENCo would be best practice.

This time does not include cover, interventions or access arrangements, all of which would need additional hours.

 **NOTE IT DOWN**

Design your own 'SENCo wellbeing plan'.

- In one column, list the pressures you face most often (e.g. workload, emotional load, lack of boundaries).
- In the next column, write one strategy to address each (e.g. templates, peer support, finish times).
- In the final column, identify one person who can help you stay accountable.
- Keep the plan visible – on your desk, in your planner, or pinned on your wall – as a reminder that your wellbeing matters.

CHAPTER 6
FINAL WORDS – WHY SENCOING IS THE BEST JOB IN THE SCHOOL

This chapter will explore:

- Celebrating the SENCo role and its unique impact
- Recognising small wins and long-term changes
- Staying connected to your 'why'
- Encouragement for the journey ahead

INTRODUCTION

It is easy to be consumed by the challenges of SENCoing: the endless paperwork, the pressure from leaders, the frustration with external agencies, and the emotional toll of working with families in distress. Yet, beneath it all, there is something extraordinary about this role. You are the advocate for children who might otherwise be overlooked. You are the voice in the room reminding colleagues that every student matters. You are the link that helps teachers, parents, and professionals work together for a child's future.

This chapter is not about strategies or systems. It is about pausing to celebrate the difference you make. Too often, SENCos focus on what has not been achieved, rather than the victories already won. By stepping back and recognising the impact you have – both in small daily moments and in long-term transformation – you can sustain your energy and remind yourself why this is the best job in the school.

THE PRIVILEGE OF MAKING A DIFFERENCE

SENCos sit at the heart of inclusion. You see the barriers students face, but you also see the resilience and creativity they bring. Being a SENCo means holding the privilege of influencing lives in ways that extend far beyond the classroom. Over the years, I've had many amazing moments where I have made a positive impact on an individual and their family. No doubt you can think of examples as well from your career.

The impact on students

- Helping a child access learning through a simple adjustment that unlocks confidence.
- Supporting a student through an EHCP process that secures specialist provision.

- Watching a child move from frustration to pride as they achieve a goal that once seemed impossible.

The impact on families

- Listening without judgement when parents feel no one else will hear them.
- Reassuring families that their child's needs matter and that the school is on their side.
- Being the bridge that turns an adversarial relationship into a partnership.

The impact on colleagues

- Coaching teachers to adapt lessons so that students succeed.
- Encouraging support staff who often feel unseen.
- Sharing resources and strategies that make everyday teaching more inclusive.

REFLECTION POINT 6.1

Think of one student, one parent, and one colleague whose experience has changed because of your work.

- What action did you take that made the difference?
- How did it feel to see that change happen?
- How might you remind yourself of these stories when the role feels overwhelming?

CELEBRATING SMALL WINS

Big victories, like securing an EHCP, take time. Along the way, it is vital to notice the smaller successes that can easily be overlooked.

Examples of small wins

- A child using a new strategy independently for the first time.
- A teacher sharing positive feedback about a strategy you suggested.
- A parent leaving a meeting feeling reassured rather than frustrated.
- Completing paperwork on time despite competing demands.

Celebrating small wins is not self-indulgent; it is essential to sustaining motivation. Over time, these small gains add up to significant change.

Enable your positive self-talk to grow and then watch it underpin how you see yourself in your role.

 IDEAS FOR THE CLASSROOM 6.1

Keep a 'success journal.'

- At the end of each week, write down three positive moments related to your SENCo role.
- They might be small – a quick thank you from a parent or a colleague trying a new adjustment.
- Review them at the end of the term as a reminder of progress.
- You may like to use AI to collate and summarise this for efficiency (and because it's like having a cheerleader in your pocket!).

REFLECTION POINT 6.2

What small wins have you noticed this term?

- Were they student-focused, parent-focused, or colleague-focused?
- How did you celebrate them?
- How might you make celebrating small wins a regular habit?

LONG-TERM IMPACT

One of the challenges of SENCoing is that progress is often slow and messy. Students may not make rapid gains; systems may take years to change. Yet, your persistence shapes long-term outcomes in ways that are not always visible day to day.

Long-term change looks like:

- A culture shift in your school where inclusion becomes everyone's responsibility.
- Students who once struggled becoming more independent learners.
- Families who feel respected rather than marginalised.
- Staff who grow in confidence to support diverse needs.

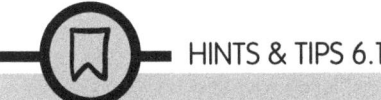

HINTS & TIPS 6.1

- Share before-and-after stories in staff meetings to remind colleagues of the long game.

(Continued)

- Remind yourself regularly: lasting change is built from small, consistent actions.
- Keep up the positive self-talk and record it somewhere (e.g. ChatGPT projects) to replay on more challenging days.

STAYING CONNECTED TO YOUR 'WHY'

In the midst of deadlines and demands, it is easy to lose sight of why you became a SENCo. Returning to your purpose is grounding. For some, the 'why' is personal – perhaps linked to their own child, a family member, or a student who left a lasting impression. For others, it is rooted in a belief that every child deserves equity in education. Whatever your 'why', reconnecting with it can give you strength when energy runs low.

 **REFLECTION POINT 6.3**

What is your 'why' for being a SENCo?

- Write it down in a sentence.
- Keep it somewhere visible: on your desk, in your planner, or as a screensaver.
- How might you remind yourself of this purpose when challenges arise?

ENCOURAGEMENT FOR THE JOURNEY AHEAD

No SENCo has all the answers – I regularly say, 'let me go away and think about that and come back to you'. We are generalists in the area of SEND, and although we all have our areas of expertise, we are not specialists and nor should we be expected to be.

Every school year brings new challenges – new students, new policies, new pressures. But what remains constant is the opportunity to make a difference. The SENCo role is demanding, but it is also deeply rewarding. Remember that you are part of a community. Other SENCos, both locally and nationally, share your experiences and frustrations.

You are not alone.

Encouragement comes from recognising that your work matters. It matters to the students who rely on you to remove barriers. It matters to families who find hope in your advocacy. It matters to colleagues who grow because of your guidance. It matters to you because it reflects the values you bring to education.

IDEAS FOR THE CLASSROOM 6.2

Write a letter to your future self.

- Imagine it is five years from now.
- What do you hope you will have achieved as a SENCo?
- What advice would you give yourself about staying resilient and true to your values?
- Seal it away and open it in the future as a reminder of your journey.

PULLING IT TOGETHER

The SENCo role is complex, exhausting, and yes, sometimes thankless. Yet it is also joyful, purposeful, and transformative. By celebrating small wins, recognising your long-term impact, staying connected to your 'why', and encouraging yourself for the road ahead, you can hold onto the truth that SENCoing is the best job in the school. You are the catalyst between inclusion as an aspiration and inclusion as a reality.

 NOTE IT DOWN

Create a 'celebration map.'

- In one column, list students, parents, and colleagues who have been positively impacted by your work.
- In the next column, write the action you took that made the difference.
- In the final column, record how this made you feel.
- Review the map whenever you need a reminder of the difference you are making.

A NOTE OF SOLIDARITY

Rest assured that I myself, do not always get it right. I do not know everything. Others have more efficient ways of doing things – I like to learn from them. Sometimes I change my opinion on a topic that I've had strong beliefs on for years when something is presented to me in a way I hadn't thought of before – I am open to differing opinions and healthy debate! Also, despite understanding the theory behind concepts such as good communication for SEND, it doesn't mean I have got it right in my roles all of the time. I have needed to apologise at times with a slice of humble pie and have chalked it up to experience. I've had to 'tow the party line' in schools when my heart isn't in it and haven't always maintained the level of professionalism I would usually expect from myself – we all need a grumble at times! I am human, and so are you!

FINALLY

Thank you for taking the time to read this *Little Guide*. My hope is that this book has given you both practical strategies and the reassurance that you are not alone in the challenges you face.

The national landscape is ever-changing, and as this book goes to print, we have a brand new OFSTED framework and White Paper to contend with as well. I always aim to provide my audience with up-to-date information with practical action ideas on key areas.

Every SENCo has their own journey, but what unites us is the drive to create schools where every child is included, valued, and given the chance to thrive. Hold on to your purpose, connect with others, and remember that even the smallest actions can make a lasting difference.

It has been a privilege to share your SENCoing journey with you.

FURTHER READING

If you'd like to continue your professional learning, the following books offer practical insights and encouragement:

- Lynn How, *Starting Out as a Primary SENCo* (Bloomsbury)
- Lynn How, *SEND for School Leaders* (Bloomsbury)
- Lynn How, *101 Ideas for SEMH in Primary Schools* (Hinton House)
- Lynn How, *The Feelings Furballs* (Jessica Kingsley Publishers)
- Gary Aubin, *The Lone SENDCO: Questions and Answers for New Special Educational Needs Coordinators* (John Catt)
- Amjad Ali, *A Little Guide for Teachers: Supporting Students with SEND* (Sage)
- Adrian Bethune, *A Little Guide for Teachers: Teacher Wellbeing and Self-Care* (Sage)
- John McGee, *Kindness Matters* (Bloomsbury)
- Chris Dyson, *Parklands; A school built on love* (Crown House)
- Georgina Durrant, *SEND Strategies for the Primary Years: Practical ideas and expert advice to use pre-diagnosis* (Bloomsbury)

CONNECT AND CONTINUE THE CONVERSATION

- Website: www.positiveyoungmind.com
- Free resources: www.positiveyoungmind.com/senco-resources
- The Sweary SENCo Facebook Group (for down-to-earth SENCo wellbeing support)
- YouTube - https://www.youtube.com/@positive_y_mind (including a 50 minute White Paper commentary)
- Linktree (all resources in one place): https://linktr.ee/positiveyoungmind

- Find me on podcast episodes made by SENDcast, Twinkl, SEND Network and lots of other places!

Stay connected, share your journey, and never forget: SENCoing really is the best job in the school.

REFERENCES

Aubin, G. (2022, October 5). *EEF blog: The Five-a-day approach: How the EEF can support*. EEF. https://educationendowmentfoundation. org.uk/news/eef-blog-the-five-a-day-approach-how-the-eef-can-support

Keer, M. (2024, December 13). *55% rise in 2024 SEND Tribunal appeals. LAs' 1.3% success rate cost £153m. The cost to families? Incalculable*. Special Needs Jungle. https://www.specialneedsjungle.com/55-rise-2024-send-tribunal-appeals-cost-families-incalculable/

Lee, H. (1960). *To Kill a Mockingbird*. J. B. Lippincott & Co.

Maxwell, J.C. (1989). *Be a People Person: Effective Leadership Through Interpersonal Relationships*. Victor Books.

INDEX